AS Level Microeconomics Revision Book

A condensed explanation of the theories and economic knowledge needed for AS Level (Year 1) Microeconomics.

Written by Abigail Barber

© 2016 Abigail Barber. All rights reserved.
ISBN 978-1-326-75413-6

Introduction

The purpose of this book is to provide a student's condensed explanation of the theories and economic knowledge needed for AS Level Microeconomics. It was aimed to be a simplistic series of short explanations of these core sections of the course to be able to build a strong base knowledge.

This revision book is written by an A2 Level Economics student, hoping to progress onto degree level. Therefore, any mistakes/'wishy-washy' explanations are deeply apologized for. Any queries please check with your teacher/tutor and don't leave it to hope.

I hope this book helps. I would like to give sincere thank you for anybody who takes the time to purchase and read this revision text.

Contents

Important definitions to get started	1
Economic Problem	3
Choice and Opportunity cost	6
Demand and Supply	8
Interrelationship between markets	12
Price Elasticity of Demand	15
Price Elasticity of Supply	19
Income Elasticity of Demand	21
Cross Elasticity of Demand	22
Production and Productivity	23
Short Run and Long Run Average Costs	26
Monopoly and Monopoly Power	29
Objectives of Firms	32
Market Structures and Efficiencies	33
Externalities	36
The Market Mechanism	38
Market Failure	40
Government Intervention	41

Government failure   45

Welfare Loss and Welfare Gain   48

Important Definitions to Get You Started

> In this section you will learn some basic economic terms to get your head around before continuing with your AS Level Microeconomics course. This vocabulary will be vital for understanding questions and inserting into your essay questions for your exams.

Economic Term	Definition
Scarcity	Having unlimited human wants but only having limited resources to fulfill these needs.
Factors of Production	Inputs that are used to make products/services e.g. land, labour, capital and enterprise*.
Opportunity Cost	Value of the next best alternative foregone.
Production Possibility Curve	All the possible combinations of production for A&B when all resources are being utilized.
Inferior Goods	This is a type of good where the amount demanded decreases as income rises.
Normal Goods	This is a type of good where the amount demanded increases as income rises.
Price Elasticity of Demand	The relationship between a change in quantity demanded after a change in price.
Complementary Goods	A good which is used with another good/service to add to the overall value of the offering but has little/no value when consumed alone.

Substitute Goods	A product/service which a consumer can purchase in replace of another, as they see it as the same/similar.
Specialisation	A firm focusing on a limited range of products in order to gain product efficiency.
Economies of Scale	As a firm increases output, their long run average cost decreases.
Concentrated Market	A small number of firms account for a large percentage of the market.
Monopoly Power	Exclusive control by a dominant firm in the market to produce/sell a good/service.

*Factors of production are categorized into 4 sections: land, labour, capital and enterprise. Many students remember these by the acronym CELL.

This section is purely to ease you gently into your revision. These are not the only terms that you will need to learn during your course, more will be mentioned throughout this book.

Tip: Some exam boards have definition questions where they ask you to define an economic term. In your revision notes, focus on precisely learning as many terms as you can.

The Economic Problem

The economic problem is best described, firstly, as a diagram.

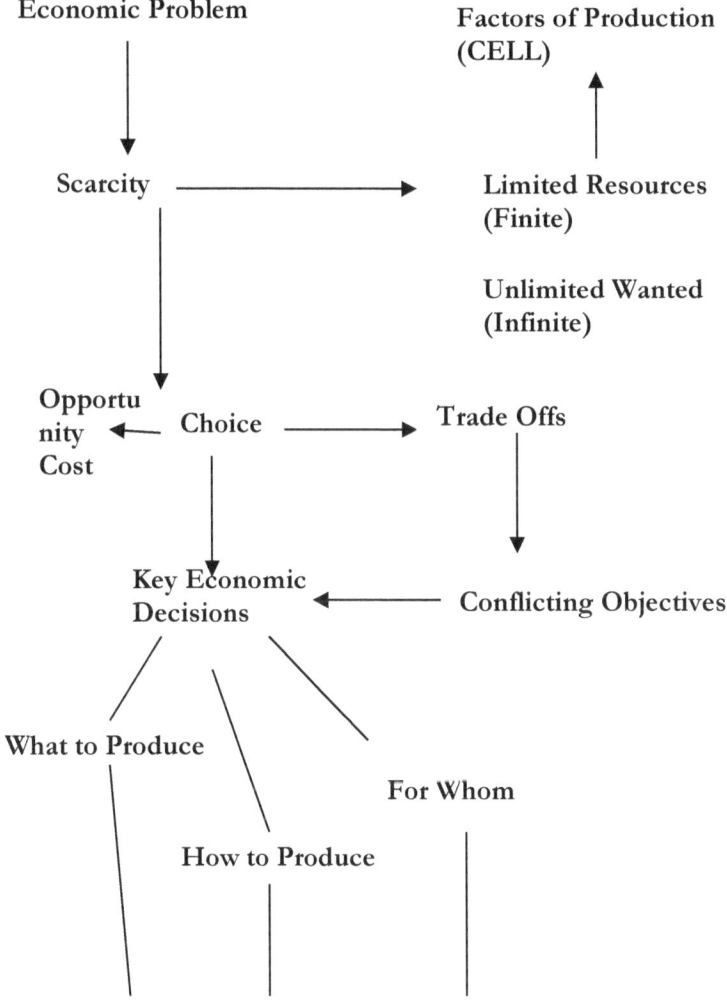

Scarcity exists because there are limited resources such as the environment and the factors of production (e.g. labour is limited as there is restricted human capital in the form of the labour force), which need to be utilized to produce an infinite amount of wants. Therefore, there are not enough resources to produce all the goods/services that are demanded. This means that choices have to be made about which goods/services to produce, which leads to trade offs and opportunity costs. As a consequence key economic decisions have to be made such as what to produce, how to produce and for whom to fulfill the purpose of economic activity (to satisfy needs and wants).

> *The environment is now seen as an economic resource as people can destroy the environment, so it is limited.*

Factors of Production

Land- The factor of production land includes the earth, sea and everything contained within them. This means that minerals such as gold and fish are included in this category. The amount/supply of land is fixed.

Labour- This category is the physical work and mental effort in which human capital exert to produce goods/services. It is often rewarded in the form of wages. The amount of labour is determined by the percentage of the population which is will and able to work, this is called the labour force.

Capital- The goods which are used in the production of further wealth. There are two types of capital: fixed (e.g. buildings) and working (e.g. raw materials).

Enterprise- This is the person who has the initiative to combine all the other factors of production to form a business and is responsible of the risk that is associated with producing goods/services.

All four factors of production are scarce and therefore economics considers how to maximize the use of these resources. However, economics has to also take into consideration morals. For example, a way to further increase the labour force could be to reintroduce slavery, so even the part of the population who aren't 'willing' to work are forced to do so. However, this would raise a lot of moral objections.

Choice and Opportunity Cost

Due to scarcity, it can be said that if we choose to produce one item, it will come at the cost of another. This is called opportunity cost. For example if you have £100 and you can either spend this money on trainers or a watcher, which one would you choose? If you chose the trainers, then the opportunity cost of the trainers would be the watch.

Production Possibility Curves

Tip: Production Possibility Curves can be shorted down to the acronym PPC. Furthermore, 'curve' can be switched between 'boundary' and 'frontier' (PPB, PPF).

The PPF is a model/graph which illustrates all the difference possible combinations of two goods (assuming that there is a fixed amount of resources). On the other hand, it also shows opportunity cost, as if you increase the amount produced of one of the goods, the amount produced of the other will decrease.

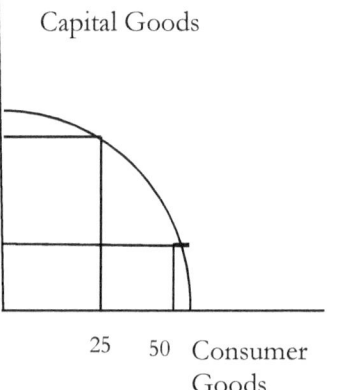

The graph shows that if 5 capital goods are produced, then only 25 consumer goods can be produced with the resources available. If the business then decides to produce 50 consumer goods, then only 25 capital goods can be made. This means that the opportunity cost of 25 extra consumer goods is 25 capital goods.

As you increase production, the opportunity cost increases

Shifting the PPF

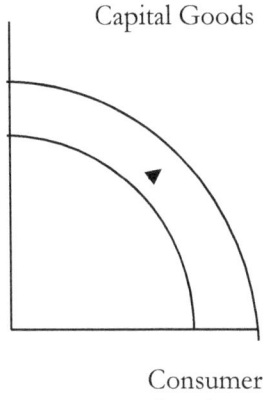

A shift outward means that the economy is able to produce more goods. This could be due to an increase in technology or training, etc.

A shift inward means that the economy cannot produce as much as previous. This could be due to a natural disaster e.g. a tsunami, or war, etc.

Tip: ALWAYS put labels on your axis.

Showing Economic Growth

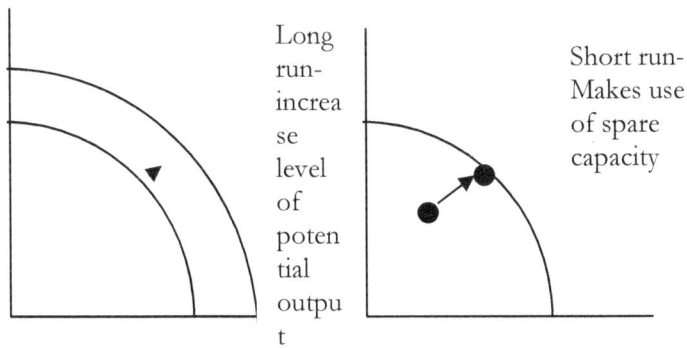

Long run- increase level of potential output

Short run- Makes use of spare capacity

Demand and Supply

Demand

A *market* is where sellers and buyers come together to determine a price.

Demand (\) is the quantity of goods/services that a consumer wishes to and are able to buy at different prices. When a consumer 'wishes' to buy a product, it is called 'notional demand' and when a consumer is 'able; to buy a product, it is called 'effective demand'.

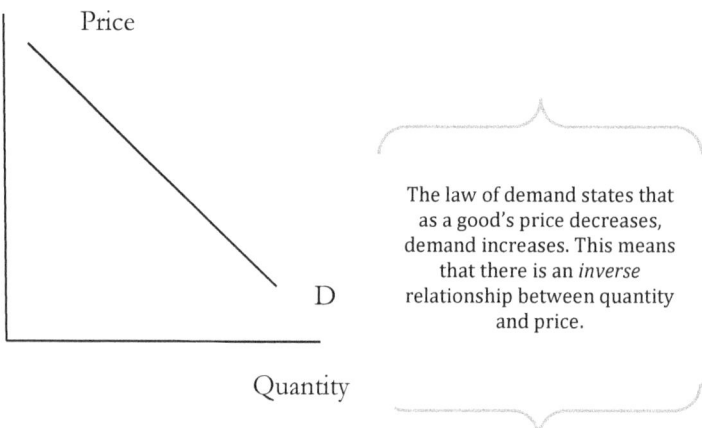

The law of demand states that as a good's price decreases, demand increases. This means that there is an *inverse* relationship between quantity and price.

This is a demand line. There can be movements along the demand line when the price of the good changes. If the movement is to the right then it can sometimes be called an extension, whereas if the movement is to the right it can be called a contraction in demand.

Demand comes from CONSUMERS, whereas supply comes from PRODUCERS.

Factors which shift

the demand line

Factor	Explanation
Change in disposable income	When income goes up, demand goes up.
Change in taste and fashion	Change in favour of products will increase/decrease demand. E.g. record players are now back in fashion and so demand will shift to the right.
Price of complementary goods	E.g. A rise in the price of petrol will mean that there will be a fall in the demand for cars.
Economic boom	In an economic boom, more people are employed and therefore there is greater disposable income to spend on goods, shifting demand to the right.
Price of substitute goods	If a substitute good's price decreases, it will be more favourable to the consumer and so they will opt to buy that instead, shifting demand to the left of the original good.
Increase in population	More people to buy products.
Increase in advertising	More people are aware of the product and therefore more likely to buy it.

Supply

Supply is the quantity of a good or service that all the firms in a market are willing and able to sell at different prices.

Like demand, supply curves can also be shifted. Factors that shift supply include:

- Wage costs
- Raw material costs
- Energy costs
- Taxes on the company
- Subsidies from the government
- The cost of borrowing
- Technical progress

The law of supply states that as a good's price increases, more is supplied. This is because firms have a profit maximizing objective. Supply slopes upwards, having a direct relationship with quantity.

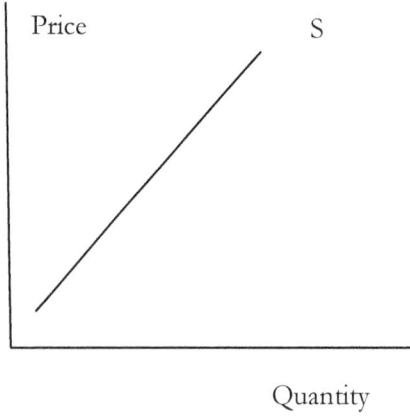

Excess demand and supply

To gain extra marks in the exam, you could include excess supply/demand when you draw demand and supply diagrams and are shifting a line. For example;

There is a diagram on the next page

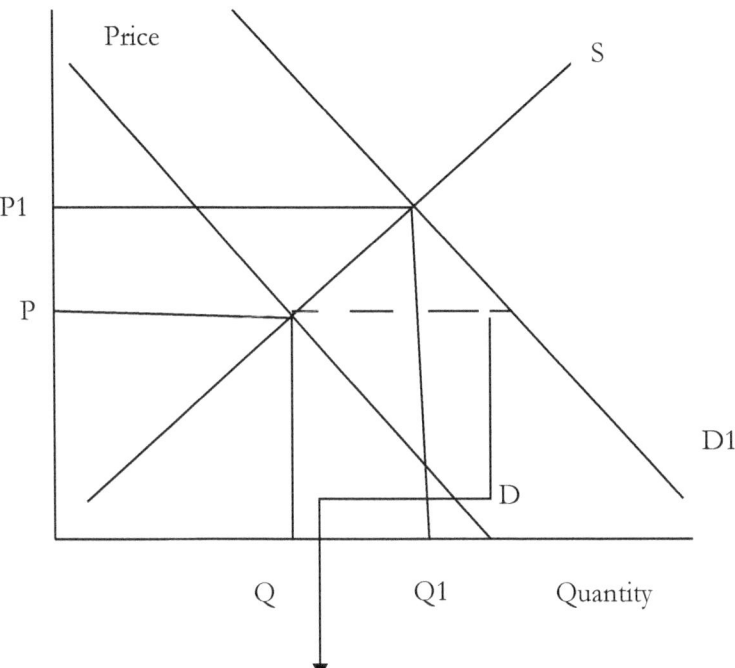

The staggered line shows excess demand (D>S). When there is excess demand, firms can increase the price as people will be prepared to pay more money. Therefore, there was a shift in the demand line to D1, which causes a movement along the supply line to a new equilibrium from PQ to P1Q1.

Exceptions to the law of demand

- Veblen Goods- These goods are of exclusive consumption/ luxury goods such as Versace watches. They are sold on the basis that they cost more than their competitors and are therefore seen as elitist.
- Price Indicator of Quality- Consumers demand more as the price rises because they believe that the higher prices mean that the product is of better quality.
- Speculative Demand- If prices start to increase, people speculate that in the future it will rise higher and so they increase demand.

The Interrelationship between Markets

Joint Supply

This occurs when producing one product leads to the supply of a by-product. For example, if demand for beef in the UK increases, this means that more cows will have to be slaughtered to meet the demand. Yet because cows are being slaughtered their skin can also be used for the supply of leather.

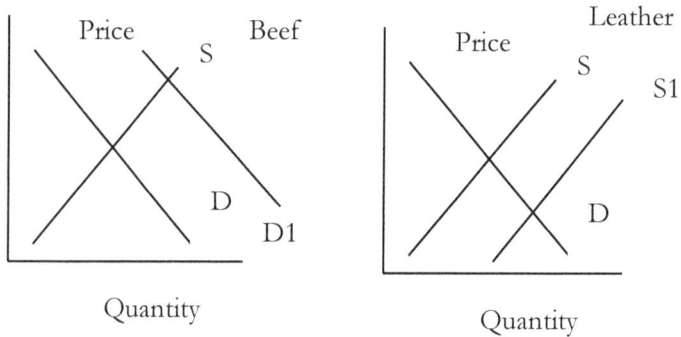

Competing Supply

This occurs when producing one good means that another good cannot be supplied. For example, this is the case with food and biofuels. If there is an increase in demand for biofuels, then farmers will be more likely to supply biofuels as they will be able to charge a higher price. Therefore, there will be a decrease in the supply for food, as most farmers will be supplying biofuels.

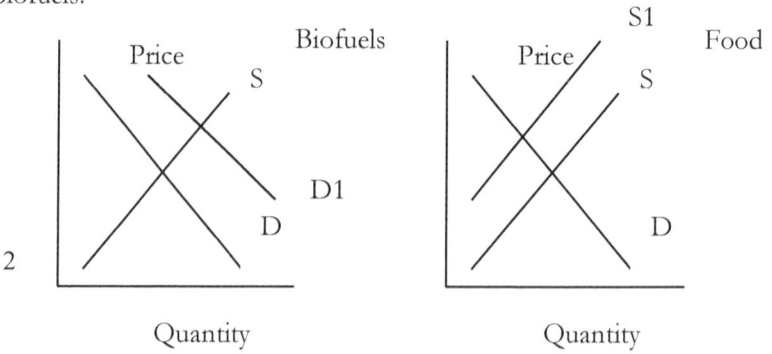

Complementary Goods

This is otherwise known as JOINT DEMAND. A good which is used with another good/service to add to the overall value of the offering but has little/no value when consumed alone. For example, knives and forks. If the demand for knives increases, then the demand for forks will also increase.

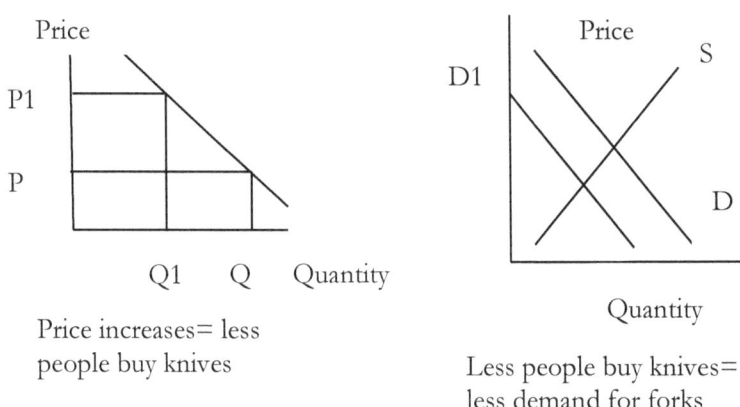

Price increases= less people buy knives

Less people buy knives= less demand for forks

Substitute Goods

This is otherwise known as COMPETING DEMAND. This is a good which consumers see as the same/similar as the other good and therefore can the consumed in place of one another. For example, if the price of Mars bars decrease, then more people will buy Mars bars in place of Snickers bars and therefore the demand for snickers will decrease.

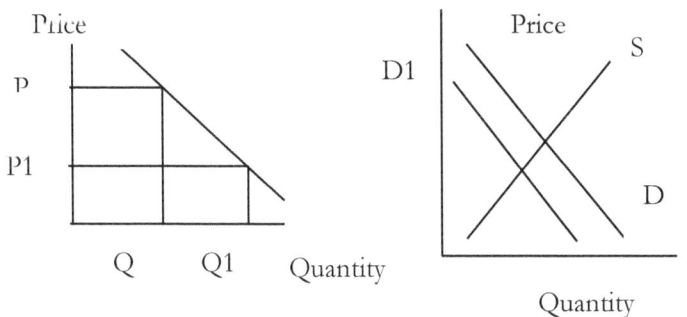

Composite Demand

Composite demand is demand for a good which has more than one use. If the good is demanded for one use, the supply for the other use decreases. For example, pigs can be used to produce bacon or sausage. If the demand for bacon increases, the supply for sausages will decreases as more pigs will be used to produce bacon.

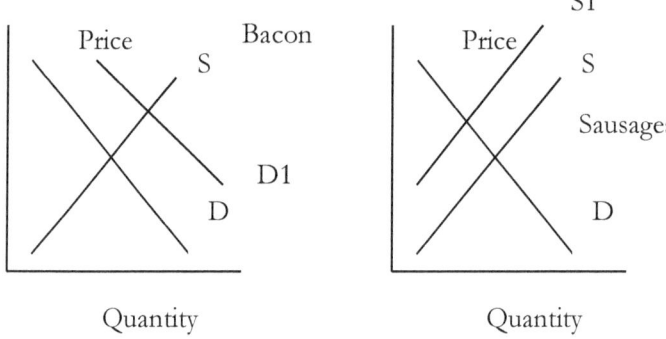

Derived Demand

Derived demand occurs when the demand of capital goods increases due to the demand for what it produces increasing. For example, the demand for aeroplane pilots are derived from the demand for holidays.

> Tip: Ceteris paribus means that everything is remaining the same (so the demand and supply lines are constant).

Price Elasticity of Demand

Price elasticity of demand is how responsive the change in quantity demanded is to a change in price. There are many determinants of price elasticity of demand, such as;

- The number of substitutes a good has
- Whether a good is a necessity or luxury
- The percentage of income the consumer spends on the good
- Whether the good is a brand or a product/commodity as a whole
- The length of time- the longer the time period, the greater the elasticity because the consumer can adjust to price changes
- Addictiveness

Price elasticity of demand is calculated by:

Percentage change in quantity demanded divided by percentage change in price.

$$\frac{\% \text{ Change in quantity demanded}}{\% \text{ Change in price}}$$

If the number after this calculation is less than 1, the price elasticity of demand for this good is INELASTIC. If the number after this calculation is greater than 1, the price elasticity of demand for this good is ELASTIC.

For example, petrol would be inelastic because there are not many substitutes. This means that if the price of petrol increases, the change in quantity demanded will not be very responsive to the price increase, as consumers will continue to buy it because they have no other choice. The graph for this is shown on the next page.

Petrol

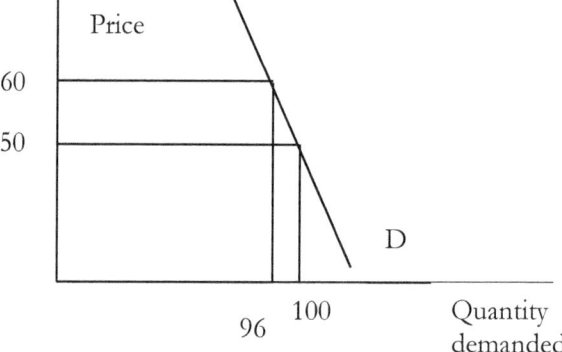

The demand line for an inelastic good is very steep. As the petrol diagram shows, the change in price does not affect the quantity demanded as much compared to the diagram below (Lucozade). Lucozade is a elastic good as there are many substitutes, it is a luxury (not a necessity) and it is a brand. Therefore if the price rises for Lucozade, the consumers of the good will just switch and buy Red Bull instead and so the quantity demanded decreases drastically.

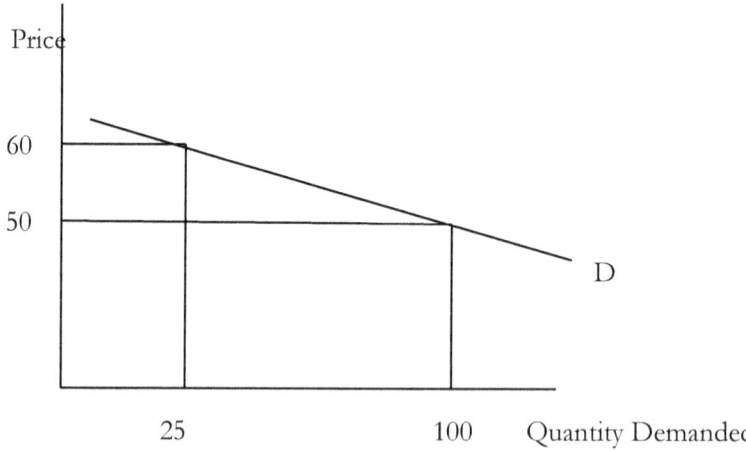

Unitary Price Elasticity of Demand

If the price elasticity of demand calculates to be -1 then it is called 'unitary'. This occurs when the responsiveness of the percentage change in quantity demanded is the same as the percentage change in price. The demand line is exactly at a 45 degree angle to the origin of the graph, as shown below.

Price Elasticity of Demand is ALWAYS negative.

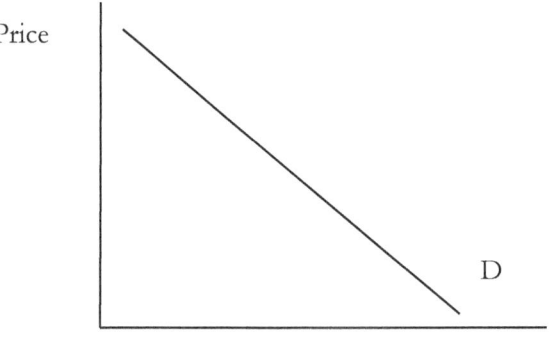

Price Elasticity of Demand and Revenue

When a good is price INELASTIC, the revenue will increase when price increases. For example,

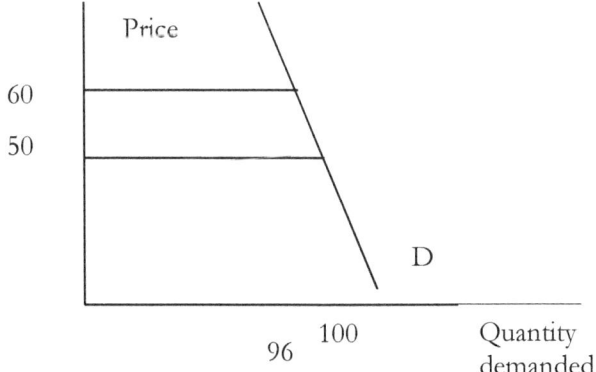

The total revenue before the price increase was £5000, but the total revenue after the increase was £5760. Therefore, if a business owner wants to gain more revenue, they should put the price up.

Whereas, for example an elastic good's price risen from £50 to £60 and the quantity demanded dropped from 100 to 60. The total revenue before the price increase was £5000, whereas the total revenue after the increase was £3600. Therefore, if a business owner wants to gain more revenue they should put the price down.

Perfectly

Perfectly inelastic demand (quantity demanded doesn't change)

Quantity demanded

Perfectly elastic demand

Quantity demanded

Price Elasticity of Supply

Price elasticity of supply is always from the point of view of the producer and is defined as the responsiveness of a change in price is onto the quantity supplied.

The equation to calculate PeS is;

$$\frac{\% \text{ change in quantity supplied}}{\% \text{ change in price}}$$

Price elasticity of supply is ALWAYS positive.

If the price elasticity of supply is less than one, it is inelastic and the supply line would appear steep, whereas if the price elasticity of supply is greater than one, it is elastic and the supply line would appear flatter.

The determinants of price elasticity of supply include;

- Time- e.g. it takes time to grow products such as wheat (therefore wheat is inelastic)
- The ease of factor substitution- i.e. switching factors of production e.g. labour and how skilled they are, or how easily you can change land from growing pear trees to apple trees
- Ease of holding stock- e.g. gold is inelastic because it can be stores easily for a long period of time, whereas bread is elastic as it will go out of date

Tip: percentage change is found by taking the original number away from the new number and then dividing it by the original number.

Perfectly

Perfectly inelastic supply

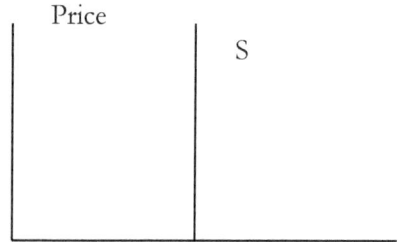

Perfectly elastic supply

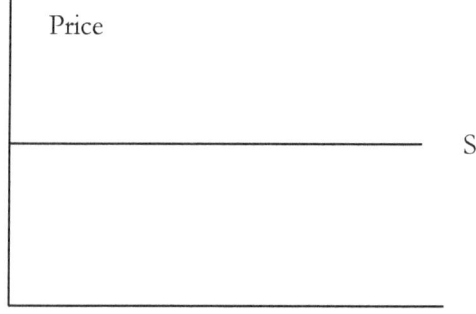

Income Elasticity of Demand

Income elasticity of demand is how responsive quantity demanded is to a change in income.

It is calculated by;

$$\frac{\% \text{ change in quantity demanded}}{\% \text{ change in income}}$$

Unlike price elasticity of supply and demand, income elasticity of demand's signs can change. If both the % change in quantity demanded and the % change in income increase then the sign is POSITIVE which indicates that the good is NORMAL (demand increases as income rises), this can be both inelastic and elastic. If one variable increases and the other decreases then the sign is NEGATIVE which indicates that the good is INFERIOR (demand decreases as income rises), this can also be both inelastic and elastic. For example, bread is likely to have a negative income elasticity because as an individual becomes wealthier, there are changes in tastes and preferences. Bread is cheap so as income rises, people will start buying more luxurious and exotic foods.

Cross Elasticity of Demand

Cross elasticity of demand is the measurement of the responsiveness to the quantity demanded of good 'B' after a change in the price of good 'A'.

It is calculated by;

$$\frac{\text{\% change in the quantity demanded of good B}}{\text{\% change in the price of good A}}$$

For cross elasticity of demand signs are also important. If both variables increase or decrease then the goods are SUBSTITUTES of each other were the higher the elasticity, the closer the substitutes are. If one variable increases and the other decreases then the good are COMPLEMENTARY to each other were the higher the elasticity, the closer the complements are.

Complements

For example, if the price for tables increases then the quantity demanded for chairs will decrease and so the sign is NEGATIVE.

Substitutes

For example, if the price for a Twix chocolate bar increases then the quantity demanded for Mars chocolate bars will also increase and so the sign is POSITIVE.

Production and Productivity

Production is defined as the AMOUNT a business produces IN A CERTAIN PERIOD OF TIME by converting inputs into outputs, whereas productivity is defined as the RATE at which they do it IN A CERTAIN PERIOD OF TIME. I.e how efficient they are.

Production can decrease whilst productivity increases. This is because a business can cut staff, yet the remaining workers are more efficient. For example;

100 workers can make 1000 units per hour= 1 worker makes 10 units per hour

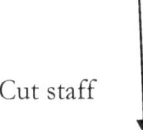

Cut staff

50 workers can make 600 units per hour= 1 worker can make 12 units per hour and therefore the worker's productivity is greater.

To improve productivity, the business could;

- put workers on a training course
- Purchase better machinery
- Offer workers incentives

It could be said that productivity is the more important of the two due to reasons proven above.

To make a production line more efficient, the business could employ the 'division of labour' where each employee performs one specific task to gain 'specialisation'. It is more efficient because the employees learn to complete the task quicker and of a higher standard whilst saving time by not having to move between work desks. Adam Smith was the first to employ division of labour in a pin factory.

Short run production is defined as a business adding variable factors of production e.g. labour onto fixed factors of production e.g. machinery. This could lead to 'diminishing returns to scale'. This is when there is a fixed factor of production and so the marginal revenue falls as output increases. For example;

- Worker 1= 80 units of good
- Worker 2= 85 units
- Worker 3= 90 units
- Worker 4= 75 units
- Worker 5= 70 units
- Worker 6= 70 units
- Worker 7= 60 units

This could be because the fixed factor of production is machinery so once all 4 machines are taken up by the first 4 workers and therefore all the other workers have to wait until a machine is free, decreasing their productivity. A firm should stop employing workers when cost equals revenue.

Long run production is when a firm can add both variable and fixed factors of production. For example, in the short run machinery is a fixed factor of production, but as a firm grows in the long run they will be able to afford to buy more and better machinery.

For countries/firms taking part in the division of labour, a system of exchange is vital. E.g. If Zambia only supplies copper, they have to trade and exchange to exist in society (to have food, clothes, etc).

> *Break even is when total revenue equal total costs.*
>
> *Profit is total revenue minus total costs.*

An example of a chain of reasoning for specialization

Specialisation allows the production process to be split up i.e. the division of labour.

↓

Workers become more skilled

↓

Allows workers to complete tasks quicker

↓

Saves time

↓

Reduce costs

↓

Productivity increases as workers become more efficient

↓

Prices may fall

↓

Increases competitiveness

To improve specialization a firm should invest in capital.

Capital intensive means a firm that is reliant on capital.

Short Run and Long Run Average Costs

Short Run Average Costs

You can calculate short run average costs by dividing the total costs of production by the amount of output produced by the firm. In the short run, it is assumed that average costs are U shaped, rising due to the fixed factor of production.

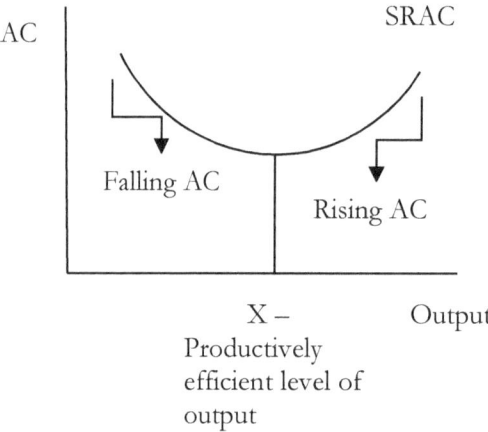

Long Run Average Costs

Long run average cost curves appear to look the same as short run average cost curves, yet the reasoning behind them is different. The falling side of the long run average cost curve is explained by 'economies of scale', whilst the rising side is explained by 'diseconomies of scale' (these concepts will be clarified later). Whereas the U shape of the short run average cost is explained by the idea of diminishing returns to scale.

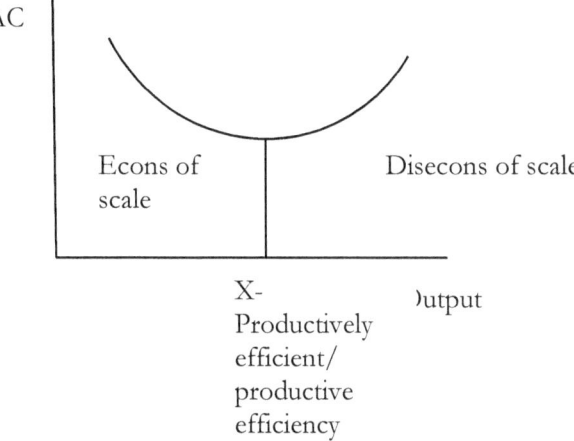

Average revenue is a firm's demand curve

Revenue is defined as the money that a business makes from selling its output.

Economies of Scale

Economies of scale is a firm's long run average cost falling as output rises. Reasons for economies of scale include;

- Marketing economies of scale- This is when a firm is able to bulk buy and therefore save money buying raw materials from wholesalers. This means that the firm will be able to be more competitive by selling goods at lower prices.
- Technical economies of scale- A larger firm will be able to afford more efficient and more progressive technology which will increase the productivity of the business, such as better computer systems or better capital.

- Financial economies of scale- A larger firm can borrow money from a bank for lower rates because they are less of a risk as they often have higher profits.

Diseconomies of Scale

As a firm grows, it could experience diseconomies of scale as the business loses control, communication and coordination. Reasons for diseconomies of scale include;

- Communication diseconomies of scale- A large firm may have too many levels of management or too many managers and therefore it is hard for the workers to communicate properly with the responsible manager. This means that problems will not be addressed properly
- Managerial diseconomies of scale- A larger firm will find it harder to keep track of who the business is employing as a manager and therefore they may employ some staff that are not correctly qualified for the position. As a consequence, the managers may make bad decisions which negatively affect the business.

External Economies and Diseconomies of Scale

This is when the growth or negative impact onto a firm is due to factors outside of the businesses control. A good example of this is Silicon Valley. Due to the area specializing in computer technology, the area will provide businesses with highly skilled employees as colleges may specialize in teaching these skills. Also the area may have good infrastructure supporting this sector, such as strong wifi. Therefore, the growth of the business happened externally.

Monopoly and Monopoly Power

A monopoly could be defined as one firm producing all the output in a market with no competition at all or defined as dominant firms in the market with a high percentage of the market share.

Concentration Ratios

Concentration ratios show the scale of monopoly power in a market. It can either be a 3,4 or 5 firm ratio.

To calculate a 3 firm concentration ratio you add together the percentage of market share the top 3 firms have. E.g.

Characteristics of a monopoly;

- *Price maker*
- *No competition*
- *Supernormal profits*
- *Economies of scale*

Supermarket	Market share
ASDA	50%
Tesco	20%
Aldi	10%
Morrisons	15%
Marks and Spencers	2.5%
Lidl	1%
Sainsburys	1.5%

Therefore, the 3 firm concentration ratio is 50+20+15= 85%. The 4 firm is 80+10=90% and the 5 firm is 90+2.5=92.5%.

Factors that affect Monopoly Power

- **The number of competitors**
- **Barriers to entry-** There are two types of barriers to entry: natural barriers such as economies to scale and artificial barriers such as patents
- **Product differentiation-** i.e. making a good more inelastic such as Apple making their products elitist

> *Saturation advertising is when a small firm cannot afford the minimum amount to be able to advertise their product and therefore cannot enter the market.*

- **Advertising –** Persuasive advertising makes consumers loyal to their product and unwilling to buy other substitutes

Government

A government could create a monopoly because they are deemed as important sectors that cannot be left to competition such as water companies. This is because water is a necessity.

Geography

Geography may also create a monopoly. For example, if you live in a hamlet, then there may be one post office in your area which owns the entire market share. It would be considerably hard to open another post office because the market is too small and so gaining customers would prove challenging.

Natural

Of course, a monopoly could also occur naturally as in the market it is only efficient for one company to gain the full benefits of economies of scale. For example gas companies generally have high fixed costs such as employing a grid network of pipes and having many companies with grid networks in the same area is very uneconomical.

> *Monopolies can lead to productive inefficiencies. This is because if a dominant firm has no/little competition and therefore they have no reason to drive down costs.*

Monopolies have some disadvantages such as exploiting consumers. Due to the little competition that a monopoly faces, the firm is able to increase the price to as high as they chose (they are price makers) as their product is price inelastic. They may also restrict output so not enough of the good is produced to satisfy consumer's wants/needs.

However, monopolies have some advantages too such as many of the

> *Barrier to entry- An obstacle that prevents new firms from entering the marker:*
>
> - *Patents*
> - *Economies to scale*
> - *Brand name*
> - *Start up costs*
> - *Technology*
> - *Predatory pricing*

dominant firms benefit from economies of scale and therefore face lower long run average costs, which can be passed onto the consumer in the form of lower prices As well as this, the supernormal profits (profits greater than necessary to keep a firm in the market) that a monopoly gains and the money it saves from economies of scale, the firm can invest this into research and development. This means that the firm can find more efficient ways to produce and therefore create a faster production line, meaning a greater amount of output can be produced at a faster rate leading to lower long run average costs which passes onto lower prices.

Objectives of Firms

Profit maximization

Saving profits or investing in new capital or expansion.

Survival

During a recession, the objective of a firm may just to be survive and are willing to accept a loss until the recession is over.

Sales maximization

A firm may need to sell a certain amount of a good to create a certain amount of profit.

Market Share Maximization and Growth Maximization

A firm may want to grow extremely quickly and gain a greater amount of market share to try and increase its monopoly power.

Market Structures and Efficiencies

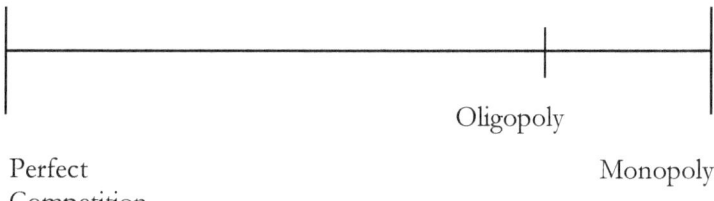

Perfect Competition

Oligopoly

Monopoly

Characteristics of perfect competition:

Supernormal profits- Any profit above the amount necessary to keep you in the industry.

Normal profits- Only enough profit to keep you in the industry.

- Large number of buyers and sellers
- Perfect information
- Price takers- can't change the price because if price increases then total revenue will decrease, so they have to take the price from the market
- All goods are identical
- No barriers to entry
- Only normal profit is made in the long run

Perfectly competitive markets are productivity efficient as they have an incentive to drive down average costs

Perfectly competitive markets are also allocatively efficient. Allocatively efficient is when demand=supply or when consumer welfare is maximized (getting exactly what they can afford and therefore allocating resources more efficiently).

However, perfectly competitive markets are not dynamically efficient, whereas monopolies are. Dynamically efficient is a business being able to change and adapt quickly to changing market conditions. A perfectly competitive market is not able to do this as they do not have the funds, whereas monopolies gain supernormal profits.

Which market is more efficient- Competitive or monopoly?

Competitive: Productively efficient-in a very competitive market, firms look to drive down costs to stay competitive and therefore reduce average costs. This will allow price to decrease and therefore the firm is more allocatively efficient and productively efficient.

Monopoly: Dynamically efficient. The firms have supernormal profits and can therefore invest it back into the business.

Disequilibrium

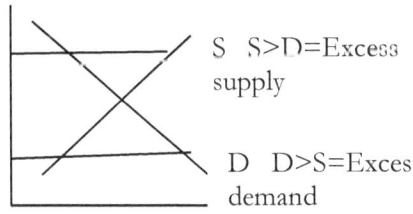

S S>D=Excess supply

D D>S=Excess demand

Equilibrium can also be called the market clearing price and there is no tendency to change.

How to improve productive efficiency

By the question how to improve productive efficiency, we really mean 'how to lower unit costs'. This can be done by;

- Improving technology- This means that the business is more productive efficient as the machinery can complete set tasks quicker
- Education and training
- Offering incentives e.g. bonus schemes
- Invest in more capital equipment
- Specialisation

How to improve allocative efficiency

A business can look to drive down costs through research and development to discover more efficient ways to produce. This reduces unit costs, which will in turn lead to reduced prices. As a consequence, consumer welfare will increase as consumers will be able to purchase more goods and services. This increases
allocative efficiency.

Exit barriers sometimes come in the form of sunk costs. This is when you cannot get it back.

X-inefficiency means when a firm becomes complacent.

Externalities

A merit good is a good which provides positive benefits to the consumer. For merit goods the social benefit (the private benefit plus the positive externality) is usually greater than the private benefit, such as healthy food.

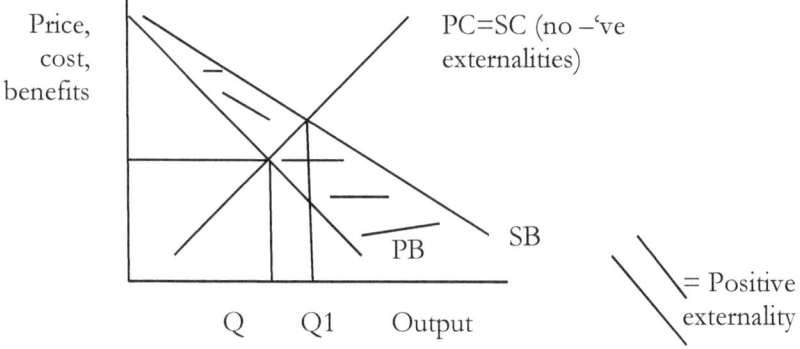

Q looks allocatively efficient as demand equals supply, but not all benefits are taken into account so it is under consumed. This means that it is a misallocation of resources. Q1 is where social costs equals social benefit and therefore is the socially optimal level of output.

Market failure is defined as a misallocation of resources. As goods could be under consumed/produced (if they provide positive externalities) or over consumed/produced (if they provide negative externalities).

A demerit good is a good which provides negative impacts onto the consumer. For demerit goods the social cost is greater than the private cost, such as high fat food. This is because the private cost was the price that the consumer paid for the purchase of a packet of crisps, but the social cost is the cost to the 3rd party (NHS) who have to pay the cost of treating obesity.

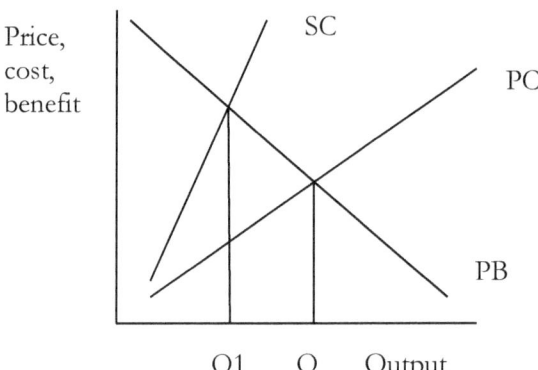

Q is over consumed because not all costs are considered, as the negative externalities are ignored so there is a misallocation of resources. Whereas, Q1 is the socially optimal level of output.

An externality is a cost or benefit to a 3rd party. A positive externality, sometimes called an external benefit, occurs when the consumption/production of a good/service effects a 3rd party in a positive way. A negative externality, sometimes called a external cost, occurs when the consumption/production of a good/service effects a 3rd party in a negative way.

An example of a negative production externality is the pollution caused by a coal burning factory in which the government then has to fund for policies to fight climate change.

An example of a positive consumption externality is eating healthy food so firms will have healthier and therefore more productive workers.

The Market Mechanism

The functions of the market mechanism (free market) are the signaling device, incentive device and rationing device. This is how resources are allocated in the free market and it is constantly changes.

The signaling device

The signaling device gives signals to both consumers and producers. When the price increases, it gives a signal to consumers that they need to leave the market and look for substitutes or cut back on the quantity they buy as they can no longer afford to buy their current quantity of a good/service. Whereas, it gives signals to producers to enter the market because, as we discovered in the 'objectives of firms' chapter, firms try to maximize profit and therefore high prices result in rising profits.

The incentive device

The incentive device gives encouragement to existing producers. If prices rise, it is an incentive to existing producers to produce a greater amount of good or provide a greater amount of services, as the firm will be able to maximize their profits. To increase the amount supplied, it could also be an incentive for the producers to employ more staff and therefore an incentive for the labour force to gain the skills necessary.

The rationing device

The economic problem states that resources are scarce. When there is excess demand, this means that there is a lot of interest for this good and therefore firms are able to absorb this excess demand by increasing the price until it reaches equilibrium. Due to the higher price, fewer consumers can afford to buy this good and therefore it has been rationed.

The market mechanism model

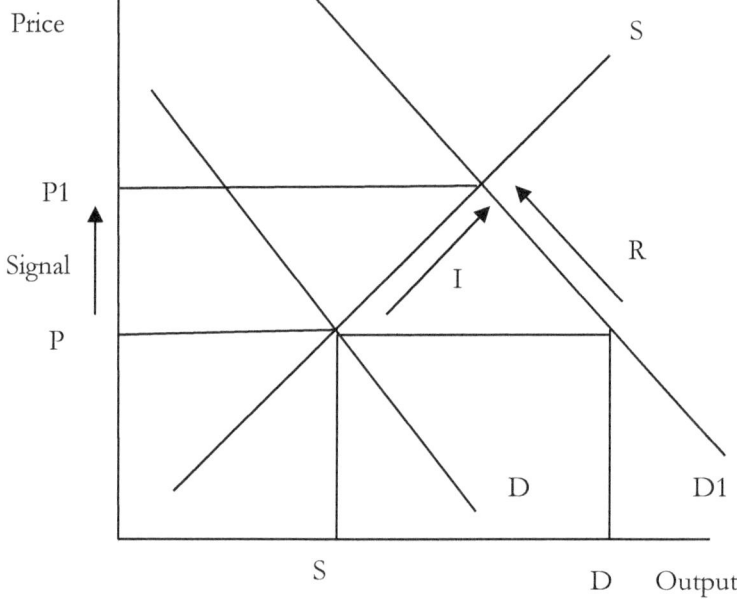

Market Failure

Market failure is a misallocation of resources. Complete market failure is when the market does not exist, whereas partial market failure is when the free market fails to allocate the right about of resources to that market. Reasons for market failure;

- **Positive externalities- MERIT GOODS-** In production or in consumption- If left to market forces, merit goods would be under provided and under consumed. (Partial market failure).
- **Negative externalities- DEMERIT GOODS-** In production or in consumption- if left to market forces, demerit goods would be over provided and over consumed. (Partial market failure).
- **Public goods-** the characteristics of a public good are non-rivalry and non-exclusionary (if it is a pure public good). Due to the free rider problem, if public goods are left to market forces they wold not be provided at all e.g. street lights. Quasi-public goods (partially) may only have one characteristic. For example a beach is non exclusionary as you don't have to pay, but it could be rivalry if the beach is full.
- **Monopoly-** Charging extremely high prices or restricting output.
- **Information failure-** Due to imperfect information or asymmetric information (where one person knows more than the other) e.g. second hand car dealers.
- **Unequal distribution of income-** Taxing the wealthy and redistributing it to the less well off parties in the economy could correct this type of market failure.
- **Immobility of factors of production- usually labour-** Labour immobility may occur due to personal reasons, transport reasons, or the cost of living.

Government Intervention

Governments sometimes intervene when the market mechanism fails to allocate effectively. In other words, government intervention tries to correct market failures.

1. Government/state provision: Due to the free rider problem, the only way to provide public goods is when the government intervenes to provide the good themselves, financing the good via the tax contributions.
2. Regulation: (NOT TAX/SUBSIDIES) Laws force consumers to consume merit good as there is a consequence if they do not. For example, if children under 16 do not attend school, their parents will be fined. This is because education is a merit good, as it gives people the skills to be a useful member of the labour force.
3. Indirect Taxation: Indirect tax INCREASES THE COST OF PRODUCTION. If the government tax a company, this increase their cost of production which usually means that they pass the tax onto the consumer, causing a market-based solution. This means that the indirect tax internalizes the negative externality (putting it into the market). This is like the "polluter pays" principle where only the people who buy the product, pay for it.

A free market economy is a market functioning through the devices of the market mechanism such as incentives and price signals.

An interventionist economy is characterized by monopoly power and produce sovereignty. The government will intervene to correct market failure caused by the unregulated market forces.

4. Price ceiling (maximum price): This intervention creates excess demand. It puts a fixed price in which producers are not allowed to sell the good or service above this price. This intervention is put onto merit goods so more consumers in the market can afford to buy the product. However bribery, black markets, etc can occur as a result. For example, a maximum price could be put on the housing market, which causes a waiting list. Some consumers may bribe producers to bump them up to the top of the waiting list.

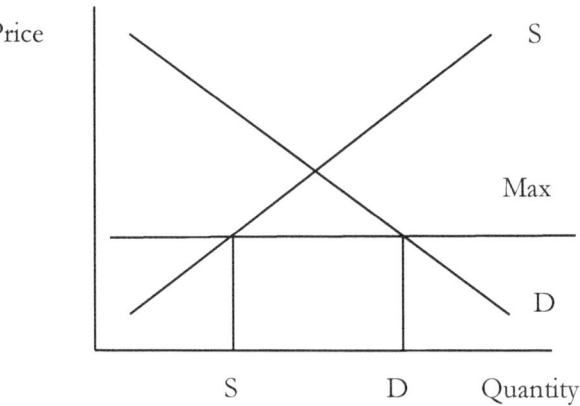

5. Price floor (minimum price): It is placed above the equilibrium price as otherwise it is ineffective as the price will just fall to the equilibrium. It creates excess supply. It is used to put off consumers from buying demerit goods as less people can afford it.

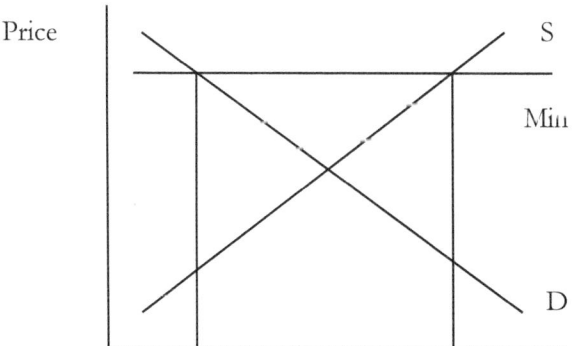

6. Tradable/pollution permits: This is a part and part legislation intervention. This gives the owner the right to emit a

certain amount of pollution, yet these permits can be traded. So it is an incentive to cut down emissions as much as possible to make money from selling the spare permits. If firms pollute more than they are legally allowed, they will be prosecuted.

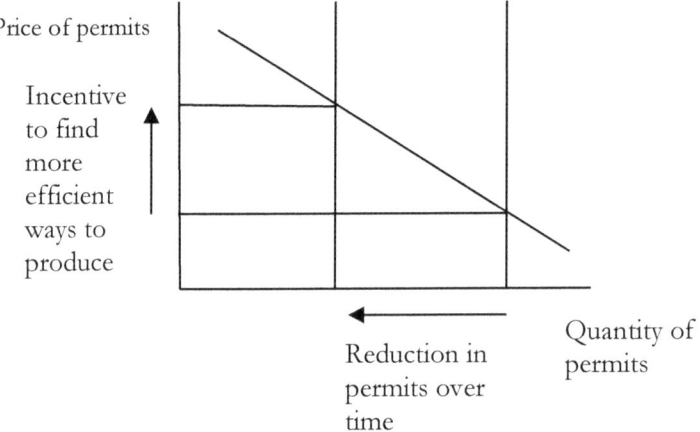

7. Provide information: Provide education as a long term intervention. For example, education children in schools about a healthy diet.

Examples of evaluation of government intervention

Evaluation of indirect tax

How effective is the tax in reducing market failure:

- It depends on the size of tax- does it cover the negative externality?
- It depends on the price elasticity of demand
- There are problems with setting the rate at the right level
- Are there any unintended consequences?
- Does it have a regressive effect on lower income groups?
- It depends on how long the tax is put on for

- The increase in tax revenue could be used to help solve market failure. The government could ring fence it (all the money they get from the tax could be put in a special pot for e.g. research and development for alternative goods).

Evaluation of regulation/legislation

How effective is the deterrent:

- How well its enforced
- Size of the fine/punishment
- Whether people except the law

Government Failure

When a government intervenes to correct market failure, sometimes unintended consequences occur, called government failure. This is because the government intervention actually makes the situation worse.

For example, the government may not know the socially optimum level of provision for education and this could lead to an over provision. This means that the quality of the education may decrease than if education was provided privately. This is government failure.

Examples of government failure

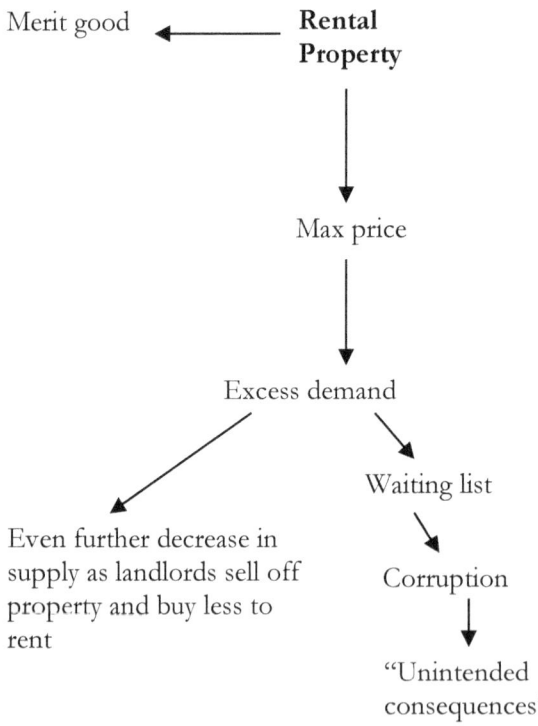

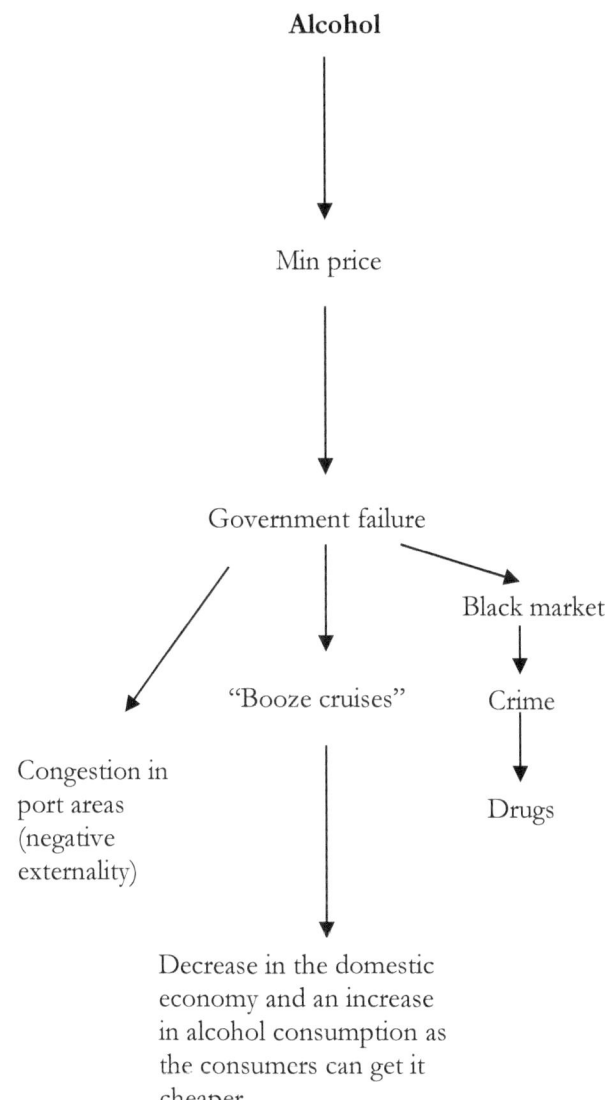

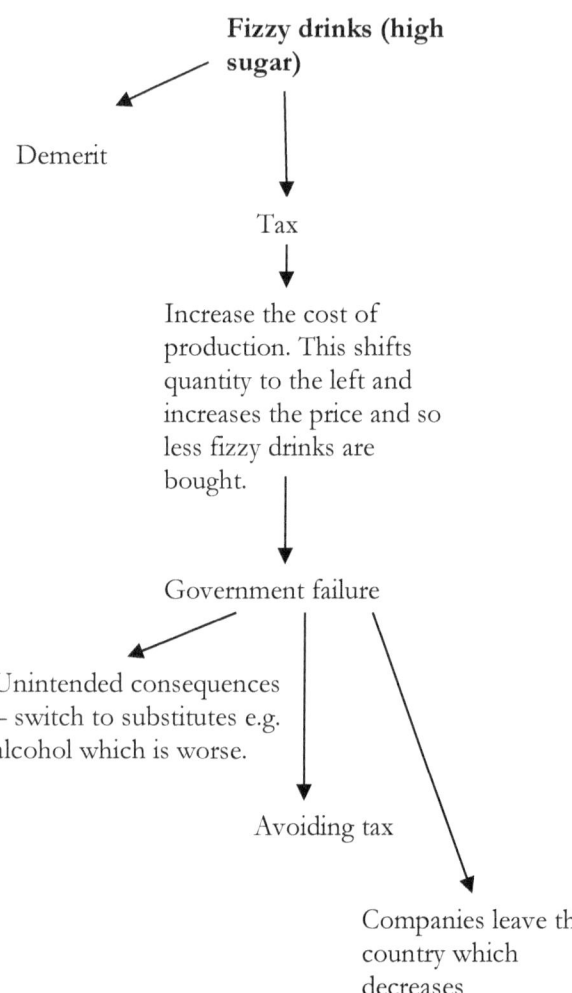

Welfare Loss and Welfare Gain

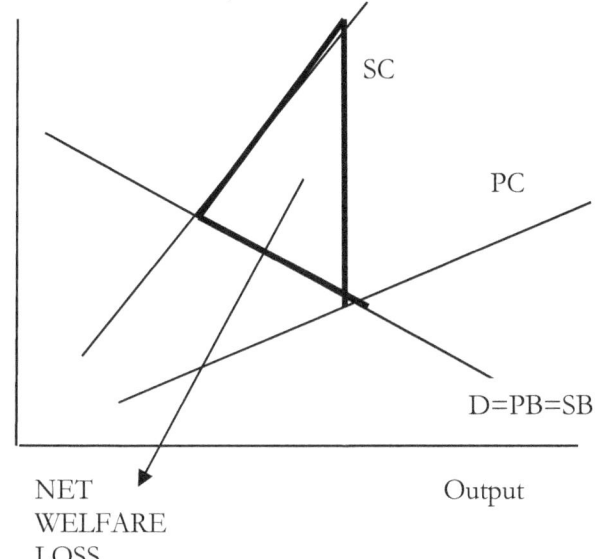

- Negative externalities
- Overproduces
- Misallocation of resources

Tip: when drawing the welfare loss or gain, start from the original quantity, draw a line up and form a triangle.

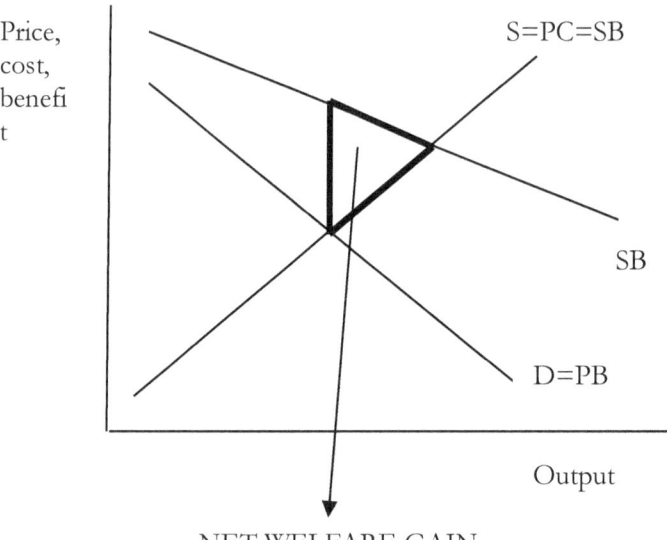

- Positive externalities
- Under consumed
- Misallocation of resources

Afterword

Thank you for taking the time to read this revision book and I hope it aided your revision well.

The reason this book is called a "revision book" rather than a "text book" is that the purpose of this text is to be a light weight, easy to carry book with brief explanations. In other words, it is a book form of what should be your revision notes/cards.

References

Bibliography

The contents of this book was written purely from my own knowledge and notes from lessons from AS Level Economics. I did not use any sources during the making of this book. However, I do know that my tutor uses online resources to aid her teaching and hand-outs(which may have been used in my note taking process) from Tutor2U and Dynamic learning. This revision tools are very useful and any references I have made throughout this book from these sites have full credit here:

Reily, G 2016, Economics, Tutor2U, accessed 3 August 2016
http://www.tutor2u.net/economics

Hodder Education, Dynamic Learning, accessed 3 August 2016
http://my.dynamic-learning.co.uk/

www.ingramcontent.com/pod-product-compliance
Lightning Source LLC
Chambersburg PA
CBHW072243170526
45158CB00002BA/994